by Mignonne Gunasekara
& Charis Mather

Minneapolis, Minnesota

Credits
Images are courtesy of Shutterstock.com. With thanks to Getty Images, Thinkstock Photo, and iStockphoto.
RECURRING – Amovitania. COVER – NotionPic. 4–5 – niceregionpic, deannalindsey. 6–7 – clayton harrison, Rudi Hulshof. 8–9 – Wisnu Bangun Saputro, Camilo Torres. 10–11 – ShutterOK, chamleunejai. 12–13 – Sista Vongjintanaruks, reptiles4all. 14–15 – Kaiskynet Studio, Mufti Adi Utomo. 16–17 – K Hanley CHDPhoto, Vaclav Sebek. 18–19 – Kurit afshen, Skynavin. 20–21 – GUDKOV ANDREY, Sergey Uryadnikov. 22–23 – PicksArt, reptiles4all, Sista. 24 – Mufti Adi Utomo

Bearport Publishing Company Product Development Team
President: Jen Jenson; Director of Product Development: Spencer Brinker; Managing Editor: Allison Juda; Associate Editor: Naomi Reich; Associate Editor: Tiana Tran; Art Director: Colin O'Dea; Designer: Elena Klinkner; Designer: Kayla Eggert; Product Development Assistant: Owen Hamlin

Library of Congress Cataloging-in-Publication Data is available at www.loc.gov or upon request from the publisher.

ISBN: 979-8-88916-576-7 (hardcover)
ISBN: 979-8-88916-581-1 (paperback)
ISBN: 979-8-88916-585-9 (ebook)

© 2024 BookLife Publishing
This edition is published by arrangement with BookLife Publishing.

North American adaptations © 2024 Bearport Publishing Company. All rights reserved. No part of this publication may be reproduced in whole or in part, stored in any retrieval system, or transmitted in any form or by any means, electronic, mechanical, photocopying, recording, or otherwise, without written permission from the publisher.

For more information, write to Bearport Publishing, 5357 Penn Avenue South, Minneapolis, MN 55419.

CONTENTS

Welcome to the World of Predators.... 4
Nightmarish Nile Crocodiles.......... 6
Dreadful Central Bearded Dragons ... 8
Awful Green Anacondas............10
Terrible Alligator Snapping Turtles ...12
Powerful Reticulated Pythons 14
Mean Gila Monsters................16
Killer King Cobras 18
Deadly Komodo Dragons 20
Ruthless and Lethal 22
Glossary........................24
Index..........................24

WELCOME TO THE WORLD OF PREDATORS

Different animals have different ways of eating.

Predators are animals that hunt other animals for food.

Some reptiles are powerful predators. Prey does not stand a chance against these **cold-blooded** animals!

Get ready to meet **ruthless** reptiles.

NIGHTMARISH NILE CROCODILES

Nile crocodiles are apex predators. There are no other animals that hunt them for food.

Nile crocodiles hunt with their sharp teeth.

Powerful muscles help them catch large animals, such as wildebeests and zebras.

DREADFUL Central Bearded DRAGONS

Central bearded dragons get their name from the spiky scales around their chins. They can puff out their scales to make themselves look scarier.

Scales

These predators hunt with their sticky tongues.

They quickly flick their tongues out to catch bugs. Then, they pull the meal back into their mouths.

AWFUL Green ANACONDAS

Green anacondas wrap themselves around their prey.

Then, they squeeze them to death.

Once their meal is no longer moving, green anacondas open their mouths wide. They swallow their prey whole.

One big meal can last these snakes a few weeks.

TERRIBLE Alligator Snapping TURTLES

Alligator snapping turtles are some of the largest turtles in the world.

They can weigh up to 35 pounds (16 kg).

This reptile has a wormlike lure on its tongue.

Lure

Curious animals come close to see the lure. Then, the turtle quickly snaps up the prey.

POWERFUL RETICULATED PYTHONS

Reticulated pythons are the longest snakes in the world.

They are great at swimming and climbing trees.

Reticulated pythons can sense heat to find their prey, even in the dark.

Once they catch their prey, they squeeze them to death.

MEAN GILA MONSTERS

Gila monsters have different ways to hunt.

Sometimes, they steal and eat eggs out of nests.

Gila monsters can also kill small animals with a **venomous** bite. They chew on their prey to spread the venom even deeper.

Killer King Cobras

A bite from a king cobra has enough venom to kill an elephant.

The snake lifts its upper body and spreads out a hood on its head. *Hiss!*

Hood

From this standing position, the cobra strikes.

DEADLY KOMODO DRAGONS

Komodo dragons are the largest lizards in the world. These reptiles will eat anything they can find.

They wait for their prey to come close to them. Then, they strike.

RUTHLESS AND LETHAL

Reptiles come in many shapes and sizes. They each have their own special way to hunt.

Some snatch up prey with their teeth. Others use a powerful venom.

They are all ruthless in their own way!

23

Glossary

cold-blooded having blood that changes temperature based on the surrounding environment

lure something that attracts an animal

prey animals that are hunted for food

ruthless very cruel

sense to feel or be aware of something

venomous poisonous to another animal through a bite or sting

Index

hood 19
hunt 4, 7, 9, 16, 22
lure 13
scales 8
squeeze 10, 15
tongue 9, 13
trees 14
venom 17–18, 23